PAPER CRAFTS

John Lancaster

Consultant: Henry Pluckrose

Photography: Chris Fairclough

FRANKLIN WATTS
London/New York/Sydney/Toronto

Franklin Watts
96 Leonard Street
London EC2A 4RH

Franklin Watts Australia
14 Mars Road
Lane Cove
NSW 2066

ISBN: Paperback edition 0 7496 0485 9
Hardback edition 0 86313 896 9

Paperback edition 1991

Hardback edition published
in the Fresh Start series.

Design: K & Co
Typeset by Lineage Ltd,
Watford, England

Editor: Jenny Wood

Printed in Belgium

Acknowledgement
It gives me a great deal of pleasure to express my thanks to Mrs. Joan Gaunt for her help in the preparation of this book, as well as to Jane Mansfield who produces handmade papers in her workshop at Pentrecagal near Newcastle Emlyn in Wales. Jane sells small sheets of her papers – a few of which appear in one of the illustrations in this book, and demonstrates her papermaking techniques to visitors who are welcomed at her workshop. Henry Pluckrose and Chris Fairclough also have my thanks for their invaluable help.

John Lancaster

Contents

Equipment and materials

This book describes activities which use the following:

Bench (or work table, covered with a plastic sheet, old blanket or newspaper)
Ball (rubber – small football)
Brass or aluminium braces (four 'L-shaped', size 2.5cm (1″) or similar, and screws)
Card (various kinds, including waste card)
Cardboard boxes (in which to store your equipment and paper)
Cocktail stick
Cold water dyes
Cork tile (or a 30cm x 30cm (12″ x 12″) felt or carpet square)
Darning needle
Drawing pins (or a staple gun and staples)
Felt-tipped pens
Flower heads (also some petals, leaves and grasses)
Fork
Hammer
Jam jar (old)
Kitchen towels
Lemon
Nail (2.5cm or 5cm, 1″ or 2″)
Net curtain (or nylon material with fine or textured mesh)
Paint (water-based, or crayons)
Paintbrushes (No 5 or No 7 watercolour brushes, and household paintbrushes)
Paper (a range of papers, including bought and scrap papers)
Pencil (HB or similar)
Petroleum jelly (sold under the trade name 'Vaseline')
Plastic bowl (for mixing paste)
Plastic buckets
Plastic washing-up bowl
Ruler (metal for use in cutting, and wooden)
Scissors
Screwdriver
Seeds (a variety of flower seeds, coffee grains, tea leaves, etc)
Shirt (or overall or smock)
Sponge
Spoons (a wooden spoon or strong stick for stirring, and an old metal spoon)
Stanley knife
Sticky tape
String
Wallpaper paste
Water
Wire baking tray (or similar wire object)
Wood (lengths of soft wood for making a mould, see pages 20-22)

Getting ready

What is paper?

Paper is a material we take very much for granted. We write, draw or paint on paper. When we go shopping, the articles we buy are usually put into paper bags. The books we read are printed on paper. How could we do without this simple yet special material?

It is thought that the art of paper-making originated in China two or three centuries before the birth of Christ. The name 'paper' comes from the flat sheets which the Arab peoples of the Middle Eastern countries made from the stalks of the papyrus plant.

This book will show you one simple way of making your own paper from simple materials and with basic equipment. By making paper you will gain an understanding of the material itself and the process of its manufacture. You will then be shown how to use paper in different ways. This means that you will be able to experiment inventively in creating patterns, pictures and designs.

Some hints

Cover your bench or work table with a large plastic sheet, an old blanket or sheets of newspaper.

Cover yourself, too, with an old shirt, smock or overall.

Have ready your basic kit of materials and equipment (see page 4).

1 Keep your paper collection in a separate box. You could include old newspapers and magazines, cardboard egg cartons, coloured tissue paper, used wrapping paper, scraps of wallpaper, old letters and envelopes, paper plates, kitchen towels and sweet wrappings.

Pricking paper

Sheets of paper which have had patterns or pictures pricked on them are most effective and interesting to look at. What you do is make small holes through the paper so that when you hold it up, the light hits the punctured areas and any parts of the surface which are raised.

You will need sheets of paper, a cork tile (or similar) on which to place your paper, a hammer, a nail, other pointed tools such as a screwdriver, darning needle, cocktail stick or pair of scissors, a pencil and a ruler.

1 Using the hammer and nail, make some holes in a sheet of paper. Go on to experiment with the other pointed tools.

2 With the pencil (or felt-tipped pen) and the ruler, draw a series of straight lines across a sheet of paper.

3 Punch holes along these lines with the screwdriver. Leave spaces between the holes.

4 Draw freehand a series of circular shapes on another sheet of paper. With the screwdriver, prick holes through the paper along the lines you have drawn. Now turn the paper over to obtain a 'reversed pattern' effect.

5 Try painting the holes in some of your designs with a small brush and brightly-coloured paint.

6 Use a fork to see what kind of punctured holes it makes.

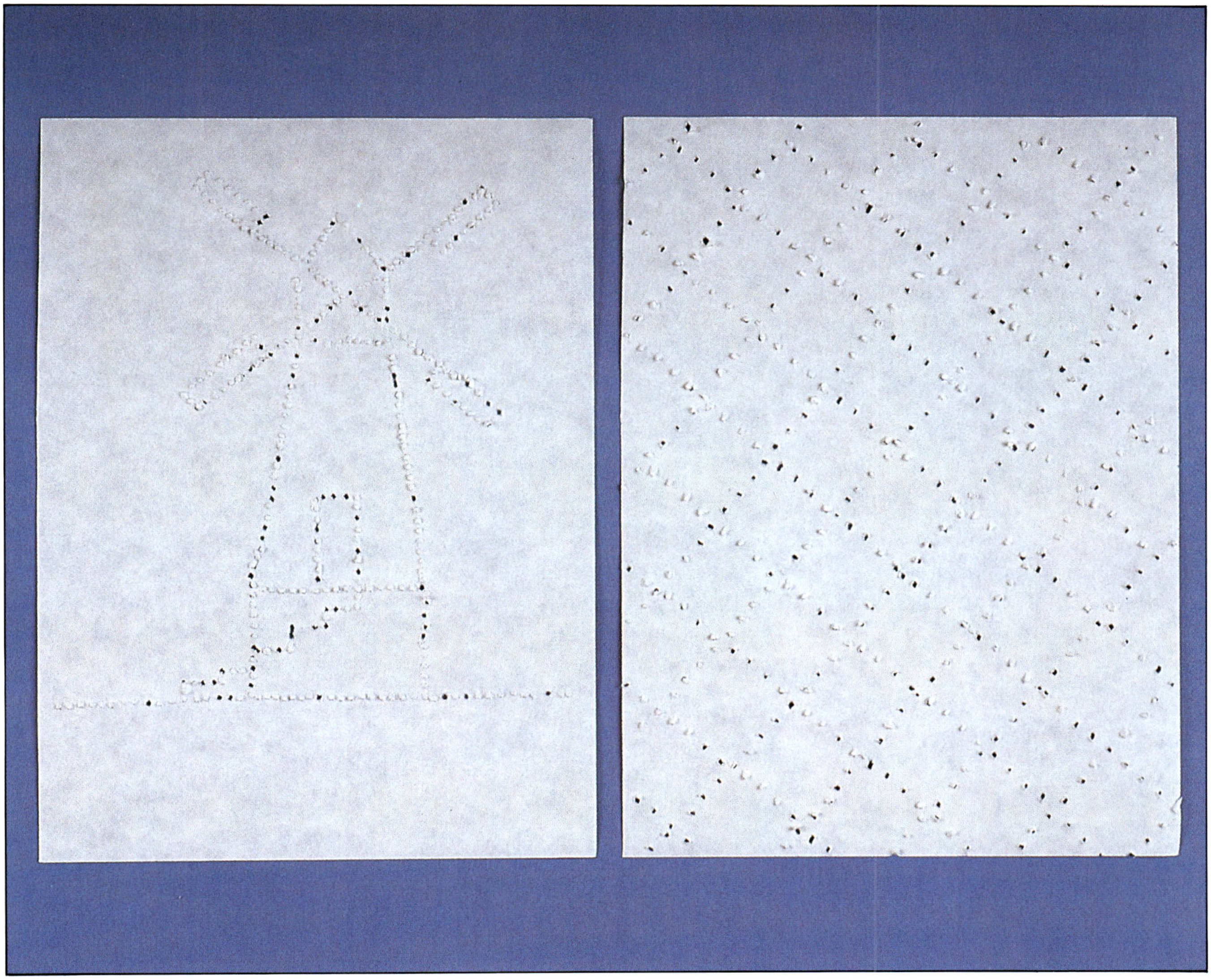

7 Examples of pricked-paper patterns.

On a clean, brightly-coloured piece of paper, make a great number of holes. Some of these could be fine holes (done with a needle) while others could be bolder (done with a screwdriver or nail), but they must be done in a 'freehand' way. Hold your punctured paper pattern up to a light or a window. Try using coloured tissue paper or coloured cellophanes (toffee papers would do nicely) to make your pattern more interesting.

Tearing paper

Paper may be torn in a simple, freehand way. This produces 'odd' shapes.

You will need a variety of types of paper, card, glue and a ruler.

1 Practise tearing various paper shapes of different sizes. These might include: shapes which are square; shapes which are very long and narrow; and shapes which are circular.

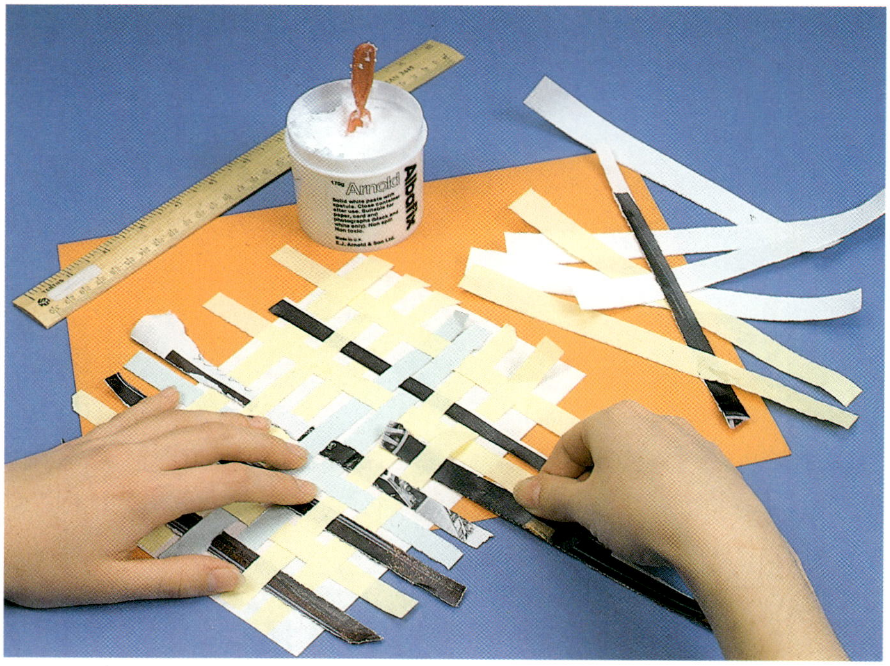

2 Tear some long, thin strips of paper and glue these down on to a piece of card to form an interlacing pattern.

3 To ensure that this pattern is effective, use different coloured papers or coloured illustrations from magazines.

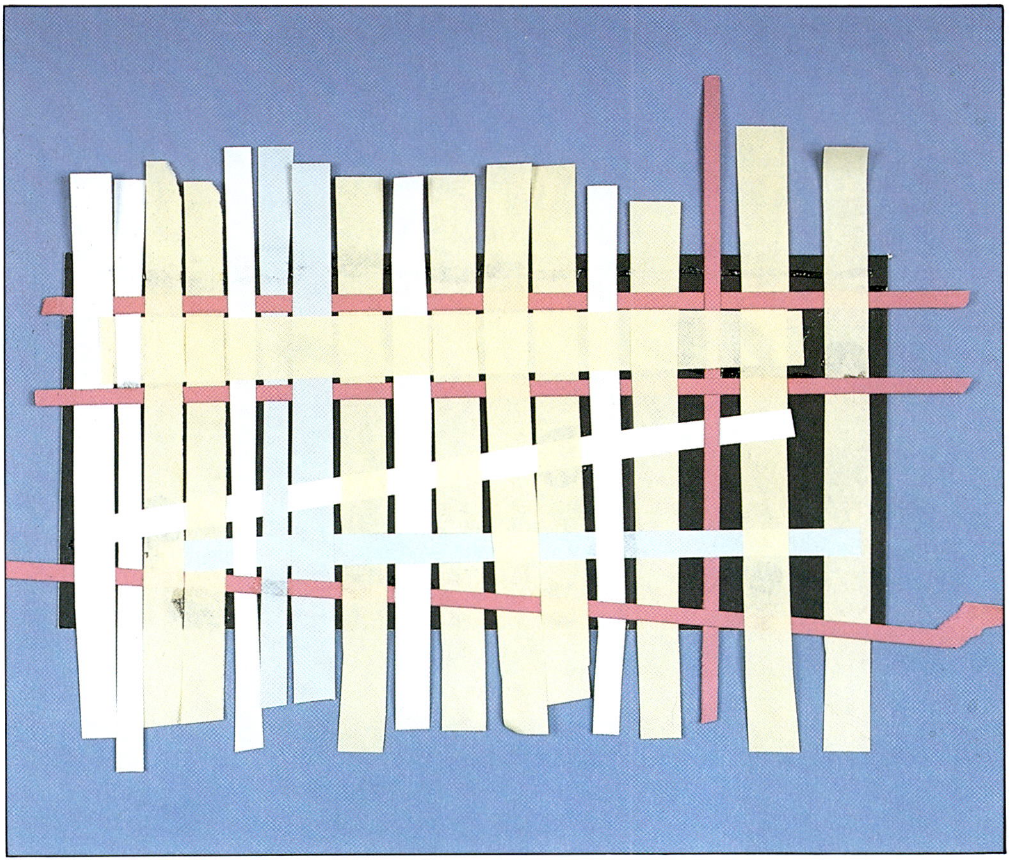

4 *A useful hint*
In order to tear long, straight paper strips, lay your sheet of paper flat on your table or bench. Place the ruler on the paper where you intend to make the tear. Holding the ruler steady with one hand, pull the paper towards and against the ruler with your other hand.

Using different coloured papers, try making paper collage pictures of, for example, a tree, a clown or a tractor.

Crumpling paper

Almost any kind of paper may be crumpled in the hands. This is an effective way of producing interestingly textured areas for use in collage pictures or patterns.

You will need a variety of types of paper, card, glue, crayons or paints, a paintbrush, a jar of water, newspaper, heavy books, cold coffee, dye and kitchen towels.

1 Crumple a piece of paper firmly in your hands.

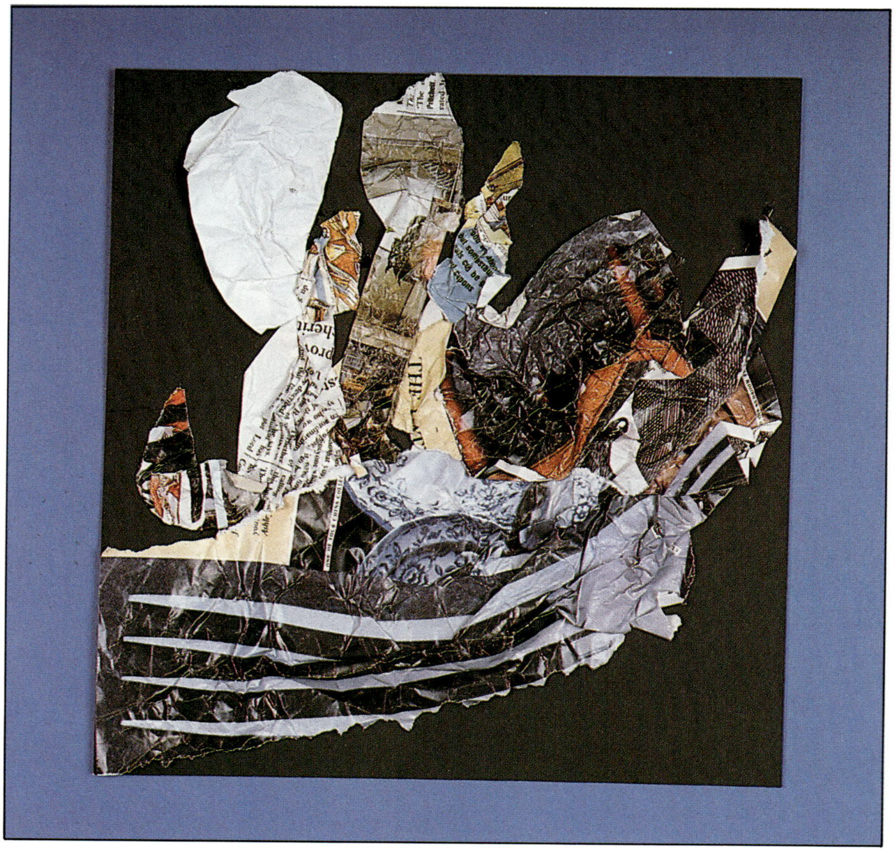

2 Unfold the paper and stick the top edge to a piece of card. Push the rest of the paper around to form an interesting shape. Glue the rest of the paper down as well, in your chosen pattern.

3 Colour a sheet of paper with streaky marks, using crayons or dryish paint.

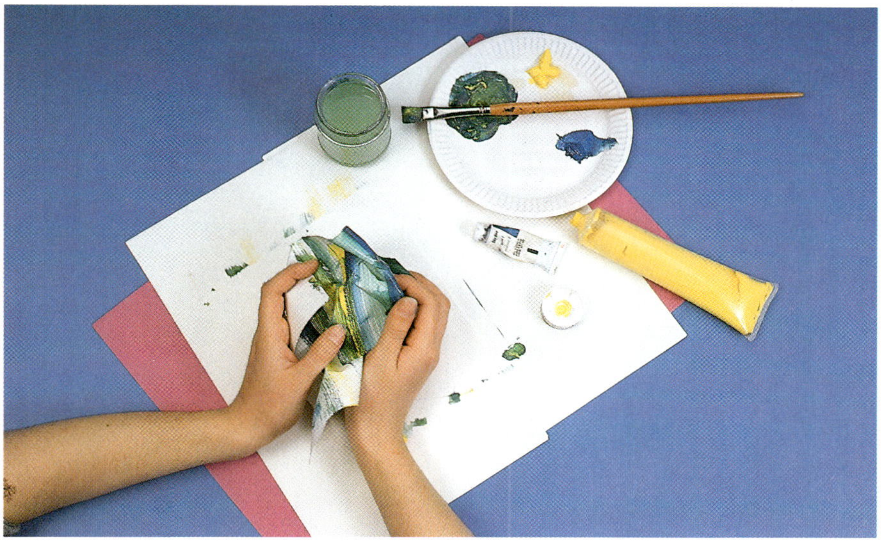

4 Take this sheet and crumple it in your hands. Now crumple it twice more. This should give you a softer effect.

Another idea is to take three pieces of quite different types of paper and crumple each one firmly. Tear them into two or three pieces so that you have a number of smaller crumpled pieces. Now arrange them as a pattern on a sheet of card and stick them down.

5 Dampen a sheet of paper and then crumple it. Lay it on a pad of newspaper or kitchen towels and place a second pad on top. Now put a sheet of strong card on top of this pad and weight it down with some heavy books. When it is dry, examine the crumpled paper to see what effects you have achieved. You could use these papers in a collage picture.

6 Try dipping a tightly-crumpled ball of paper into some cold coffee or dye. When it has dried, open it out and you will have a crackled effect. Japanese papers sometimes have lovely 'punctured' patterns and these can be stained in this way to make them even more interesting.

7 Stick some of the pieces of paper which you have crumpled on to a strong sheet of coloured paper or card.

8 You can arrange them so that they form a design.

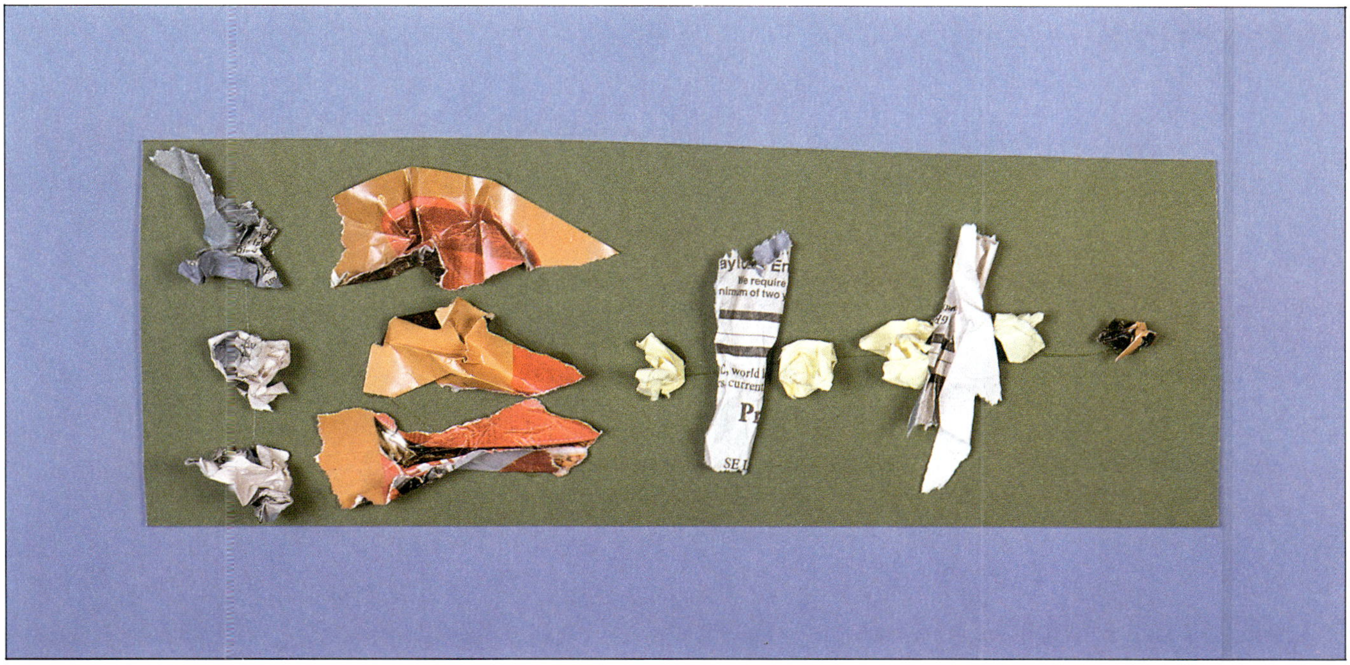

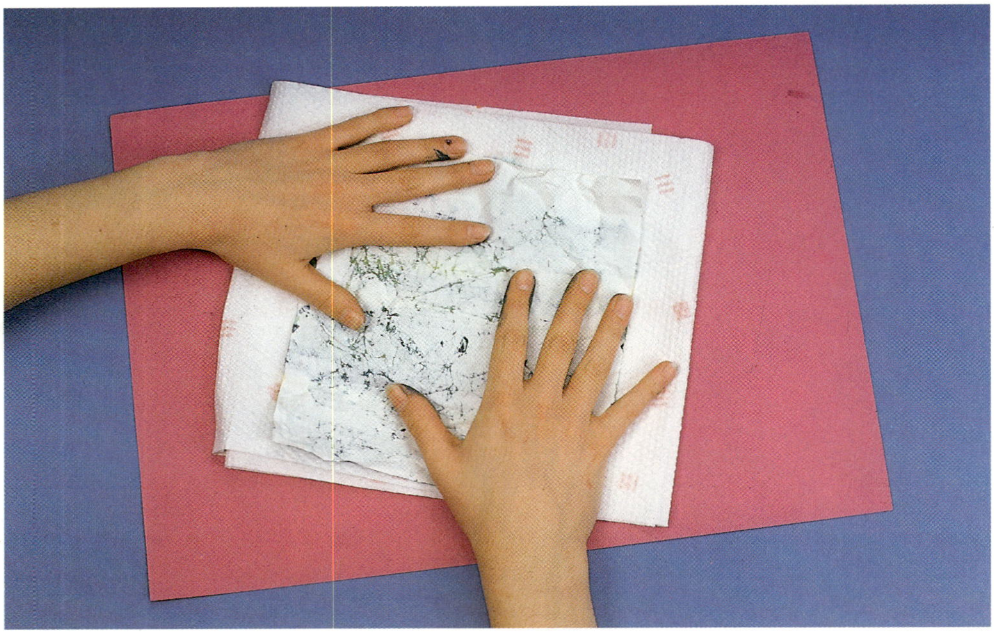

9 Make a pad of two or three sheets of kitchen towel and place it on top of your bench or table. On a stronger sheet of paper, paint some coloured dots, circles, lines or other shapes with wet paint. While the paint is still wet, lay the sheet face down on to the pad and press down firmly.

10 When you lift it up, it will leave a soft, printed image on the top sheet of kitchen paper.

Experiment with this crumpled paper technique to see how many different kinds of prints you can make.

A collage landscape picture

A 'relief' design is one in which attached materials – in this case paper – project (stick out) from the background surface.

You will need a variety of types of paper, a piece of strong paper or card (about 18cm x 23cm, 7″ x 9″) on which to create your collage, a pencil or felt-tipped pen and glue.

1 Draw a series of lines freely across the base paper or card with the pencil or felt-tipped pen. Leave varying spaces between the lines, ranging, say, from about 2.5cm to 5cm (1″ to 2″).

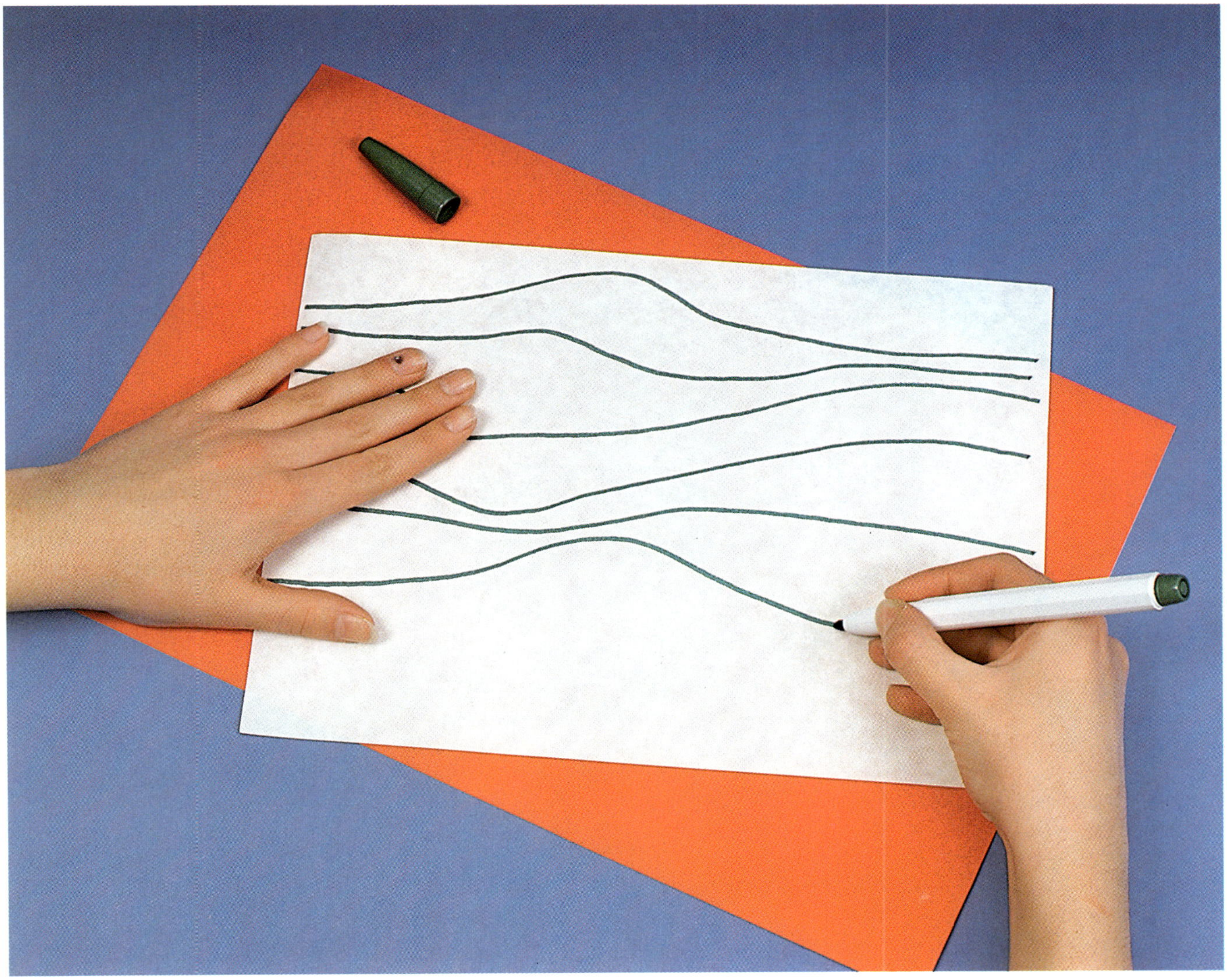

2 Select six or seven different types of paper (newspaper, wrapping paper, wallpaper, for example). Tear strips of these different papers to fit into the spaces between the lines. You do not need to be absolutely accurate, but your aim should be to fill the spaces completely when the torn pieces are stuck down.

3 Some areas could be coloured in with the felt-tipped pen, or you might even like to texture them with little dots or scribbled marks.

4 Draw or paint some trees on your collage picture to complete it.

Making your own paper

The processes involved in making decorative sheets of paper by hand from recycled papers and plant materials are quite simple. You will, however, require the help of an adult or an older brother, sister or friend with some of the things you need to do. Work carefully so that you don't make a mess. If the weather is fine, I suggest that you work outside.

You will need two plastic buckets, a wooden spoon or stick for stirring, a small wooden frame called a *mould* (photos 1-5 show you how to make this) a selection of used paper ('dull', not shiny paper, e.g., tissue paper, envelopes, computer print-out paper, paper bags, brown wrapping paper, cardboard egg cartons) and water.

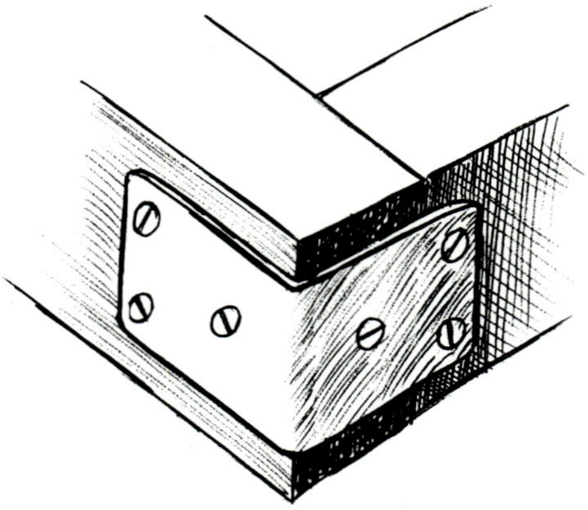

1 Join the strips of wood together at the corners so that they form a *rectangular* frame (25cm x 20 cm, 10" x 8"). Use the L-shaped braces, as these will not rust and discolour your hand-made papers. Screw them into place.

2 Now cover *one* side of the wooden frame with a piece of the net curtain. Its mesh may be fine or coarse and you can have fun experimenting with different types.

3 Staple (or attach with drawing pins) one edge of the net curtain to the underside of one edge of the frame. Now pull the net tightly across the frame and staple the opposite edge down firmly. Repeat this operation along the other two edges. The stretched net curtain should now be taut, like an artist's canvas.

Making the 'mould'

The mould, or wooden frame, needs to be strong and firm to give you the best possible results. You might find it useful to have some help in making this, to ensure that it is well constructed.

You will need a length (about 90cm, 3ft) of soft wood with a *square section* (e.g., 2.5cm x 2.5cm, 1″ x 1″ or similar). This can be purchased from a DIY store. This strip should be sawn into four lengths – two x 25cm (10″) long and two x 20cm (8″) long. (These measurements are only a guide and you may wish to change them.)

Soft wood is ideal for your first experiments in paper making, though hard woods such as mahogany and teak are better for making moulds which will get lots of use. Professional paper makers use hard woods for their moulds.

You will also need small, L-shaped brass or aluminium braces, small brass screws, a screwdriver, some old net curtain material, and drawing pins or a staple gun and staples.

You now need to make another, lighter wooden frame to fit on to your mould (see photos 4 and 5). For this you will need a length (about 90cm, 3ft) of soft wood with a square section (1.2cm x 1.2cm, ½″ x ½″). This length should be sawn into four sections, two x 25cm (10″) and two x 20cm (8″). Join the strips together as before, with braces and screws.

4 Place this lighter frame on the net curtain side of your mould.

5 Attach it with a few short strips of masking tape to hold it in place.

Making a sheet of paper by hand

The method of paper-making described here is easy to follow.

6 Tear up some of your pieces of used paper and place them in a plastic bucket.

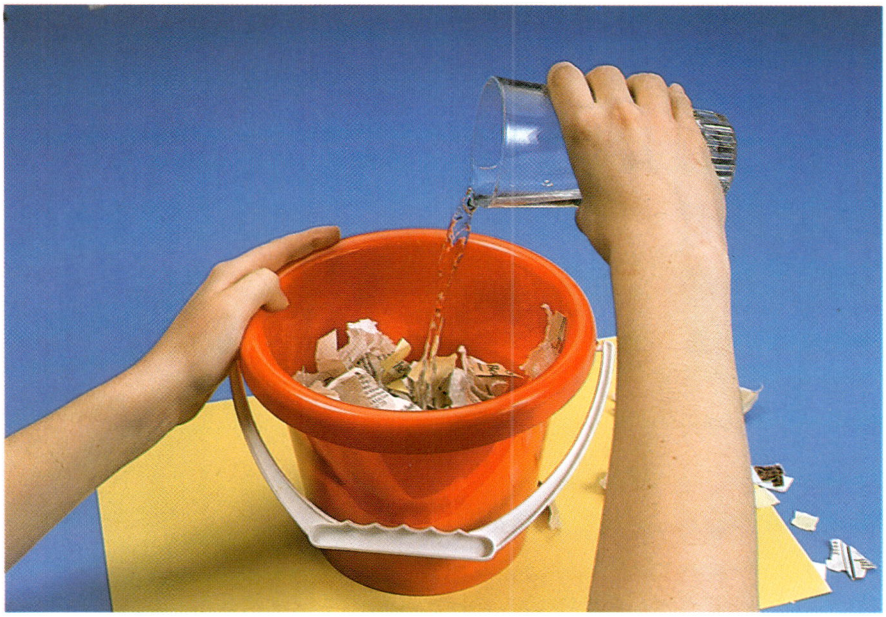

7 Pour cold water over the torn-up paper and allow it to soak overnight. (If you are in a hurry, then you may, with care, use very hot water and leave the mixture for about 2-3 hours).

8 Pound the soaked paper into a mushy, porridge-like pulp. You will need to stir it vigorously with the wooden spoon or stick.

9 Rest your mould on top of the second bucket. Scoop up some of the pulp and place it into the mould.

10 Use your hands to spread the pulp around carefully.

11 Make sure that you cover the mesh right up to the edges. (You might be interested to know that in paper making an edge is called a 'deckel'. Unlike a cut edge, it tends to be slightly ragged.)

12 Leave the wet mush in the mould to dry before peeling it from the mould. (For further information on drying paper, see page 30.)

An alternative method

Pour the pulp into an old washing-up bowl.

Take your mould (mesh side down) and dip one of its shorter sides into the mushy pulp.

Slide the mould slowly underneath the surface of the pulp. (NB If you follow this method, make sure the measurements of your mould allow it to fit into the washing-up bowl!)

Slowly scoop up some pulp in the mould.

Lift the mould out, allowing excess liquid to drain away.

In order to support the now heavy, wet mush of matted fibres, place the mould on a wire baking tray so that further drips of liquid fall away into a bucket or a sink. Leave to dry.

13 This early print shows the paper maker scooping pulp from a huge, wooden vat with his mould.

Useful hints

1 When making the pulp, you will get better results if your torn-up pieces of paper are small (say, 1-2cm, ½-1″).

2 Don't leave the pulp in a bucket for longer than two days otherwise it will become smelly.

3 Clean buckets and other equipment immediately after use.

Experimental variations

Paper is not only a material on which to draw, write, print or paint. It can be enjoyed simply as a decorative material which varies in colour and texture. When producing your own sheets of hand-made paper you can use a variety of raw materials to obtain effective variations in colour, pattern and texture. Here are some ideas.

1 Add two or three leaves from plants to the pulp as you mix it.
2 Various flower-heads (daisies, dandelions, roses or daffodils, for example) can be squeezed in your fingers and then mixed into the pulp.
3 Try sprinkling a few seeds, small flower-heads or petals on to the damp layer of pulp in your mould so that when it dries they become part of the sheet of paper.
4 Add a little starch or gelatine to the pulp as you mix it, to give the paper more body. (This will also tend to give it a slightly smoother surface.)
5 Thin or sliced flower stalks will give an unusual effect.
6 Experiment with dried leaves, dried grasses and dried flowers.
7 Sprinkle some coffee or tea grains on to the damp layer of pulp in the mould.
8 Obtain colour variations by adding to the pulp as you mix it some ink, paint, cold water dye, cold tea or cold coffee.
9 Drop a few spots of ink or paint on to the damp layer of pulp in the mould.

Try combining one or more of these ideas.

Keep a notebook in which you write about your experiments. Note down the various types of papers which you used to make your pulp; the different types of natural materials which you added; and how you obtained certain effects of colour and texture. Glue small samples of the papers you have made beside your written notes.

As you become more skilled in making paper, you may wish to try a few clever variations. Here are some more ideas:

1 Make a quantity of very thick, dark-coloured pulp. Keep it ready for use in a plastic bowl so that you can quickly add lumps of it to a thinner layer of lighter-coloured pulp in the mould.

2 Drag your fingers through a layer of wet pulp in the mould to produce 'ridges' and 'furrows'.

3 Place one or two delicate feathers into a layer of damp pulp in the mould.

14 Press and poke a layer of pulp which is almost dry so that areas of it are torn.

15 Sprinkle some delicate flower petals, leaves, seeds or grass stalks on to the pulp.

4 Place lengths of coloured wool, string or cotton into a layer of damp pulp as it lies in the mould and then allow it to dry.

5 Do the same again but this time tear away some areas of the damp paper to produce interesting effects.

Photos 16-19 show the results of some of these ideas. Now try some ideas of your own.

16

17

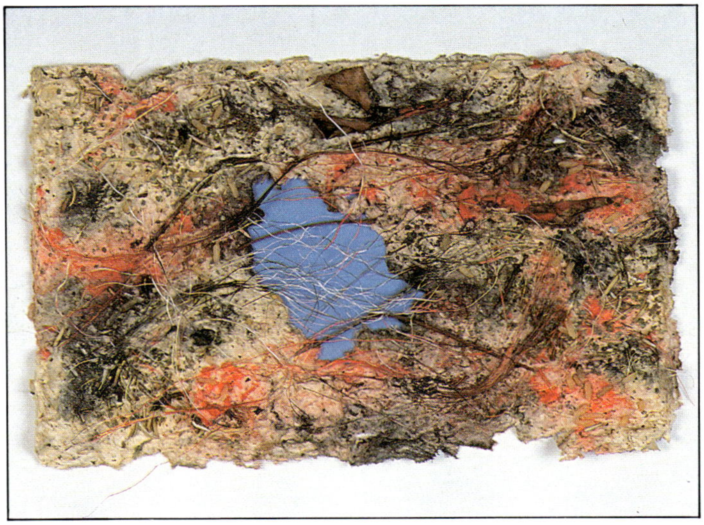

18

Drying a sheet of newly-made paper

A layer of wet pulp may be left in the mould to dry. This takes quite a long time, however, and you may wish your paper to dry quickly.

If so, place your mould, mesh side down, on a thick pad of newspaper or on an old blanket, if you have one. Such a pad will act like blotting paper and will soak up a lot of moisture from the layer of pulp.

After about an hour you should lift the mould off the pad and rest it on two strips of wood so that air is able to circulate beneath it. This will help the sheet of new paper to dry out more quickly.

The surface of your sheet of paper will be rough. You will be unable to write properly on it with pen and ink, but sometimes a felt-tipped pen may be used successfully.

Experiment by drawing and painting freely with different materials and tools.

19

Making indented designs

Indented patterns are produced by impressing objects into the surface of a sheet of paper. The objects themselves must be hard and firm so that they will affect the paper by leaving 'pressed' marks in it.

You will need a piece of strong card or a cork tile, seeds or grains of sand, a sheet of paper, a sponge and a spoon.

1 Sprinkle some seeds or grains of sand on to the card or cork tile.

2 Dampen the sheet of paper with the sponge and lay it down on the 'seeded' surface. Rub the paper gently but firmly with the back of the spoon or with your hand. Lift up the paper and allow it to dry. Use your piece of indented paper in some exciting way by colouring it with crayon or dryish paint.

Here are some other ideas.
1 Instead of rubbing the paper with a spoon, try putting a pad of newspaper over it, placing two or three heavy books on top and leaving it to dry.
2 Take a sheet of paper, a spoon, a pad of newspaper and a ruler. Place the clean paper on the newspaper pad. Now draw a series of straight lines by using the blunt end of the spoon and the ruler. Press firmly into the paper.
3 Instead of the spoon, use small twigs or cut-out cardboard shapes to impress patterns.
4 Using seeds or grains of sand as shown in photo 1, make a pattern based upon circles.
5 Try different methods, and use objects such as a wire baking tray, a plastic tray and string.

3 Tape a design made from strips of card on to a sheet of aluminium foil.

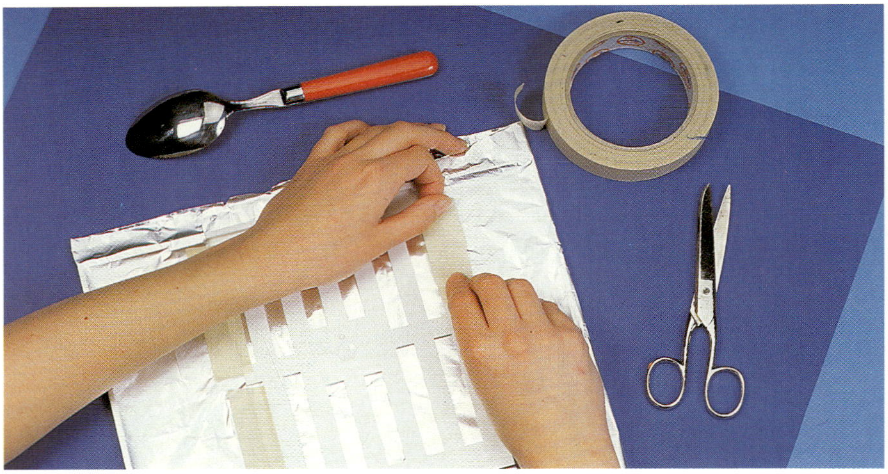

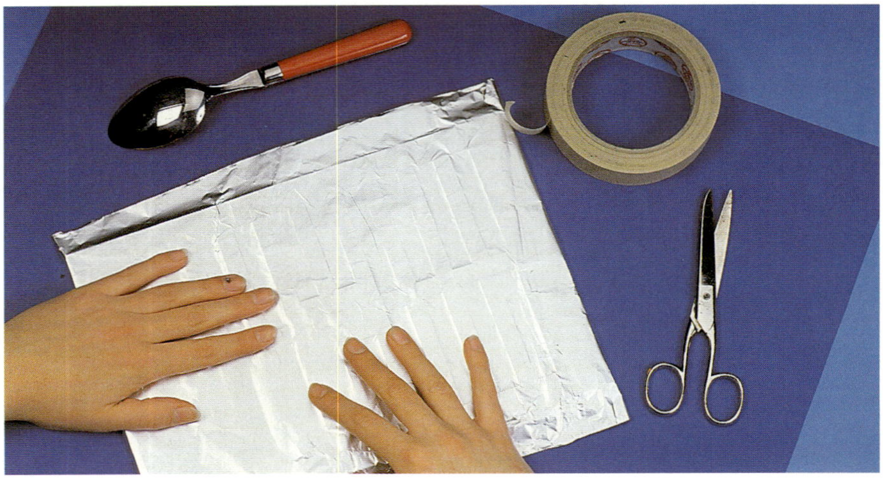

4 Turn the sheet over and rub gently but firmly with the back of a spoon. The card strips will form an indented pattern on the foil.

5 and 6 What do you think was used to make these patterns?

5

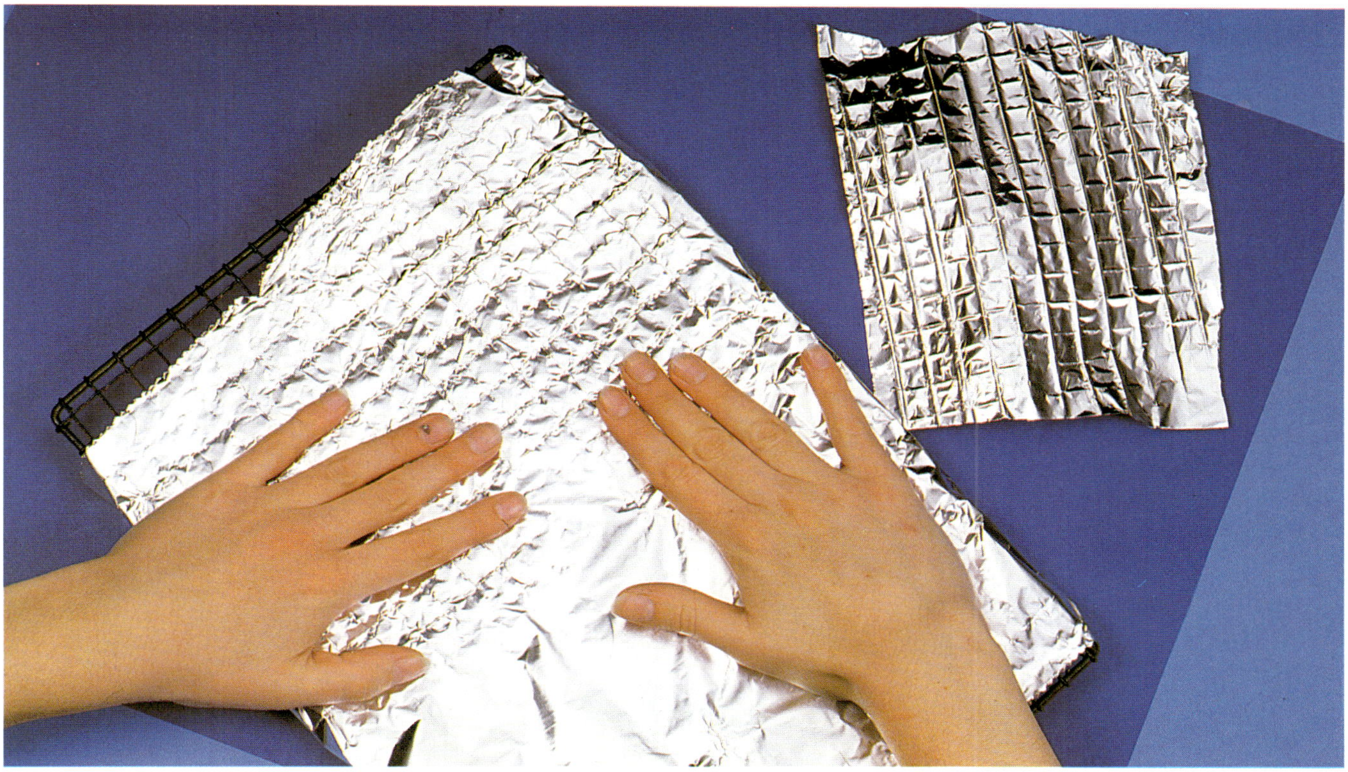

6

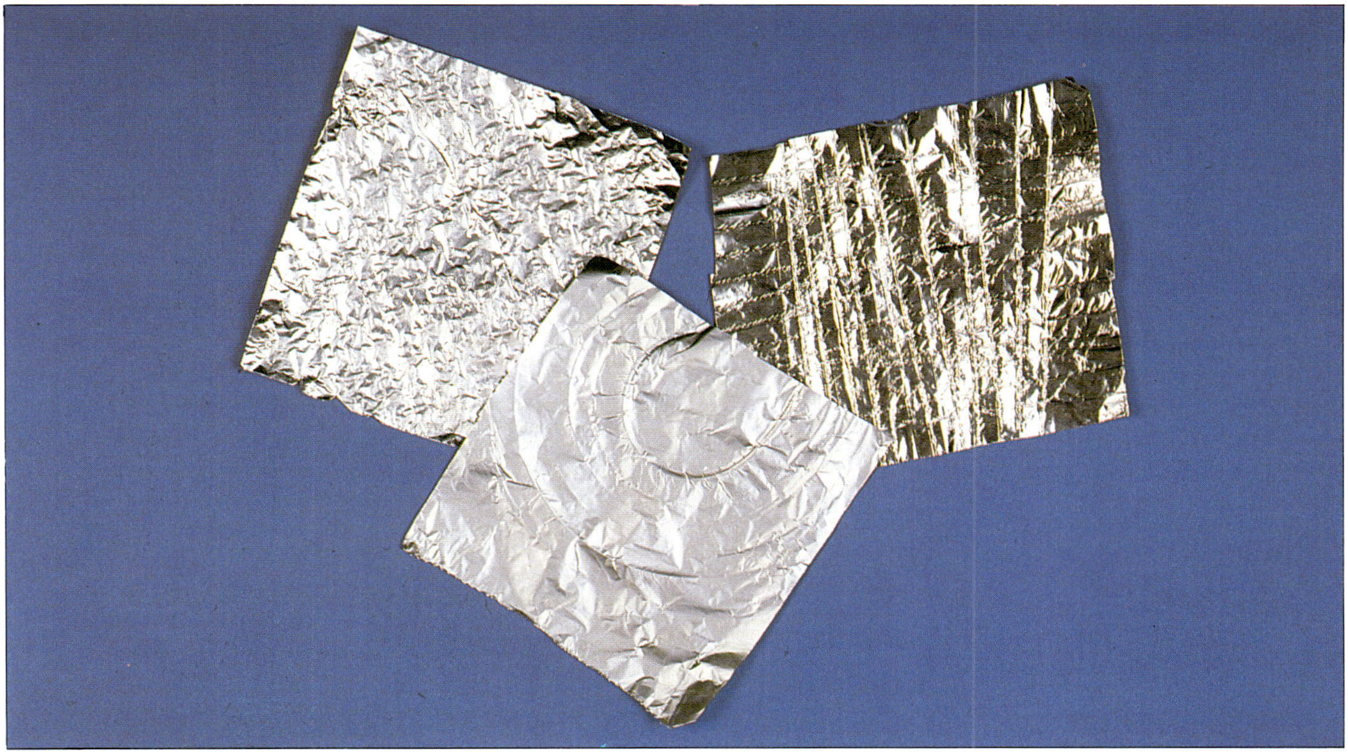

Papier mâché dishes

Dish-like shapes made from paper are not difficult to make. You can start by using a rubber ball (a small football will do nicely), a plastic bucket (large enough for the ball to sit in the top), some paper (pieces of newspaper or wrapping paper), wallpaper paste, a paintbrush (2.5cm, 1″, household paintbrush), a plastic bowl or basin to hold the paste and some petroleum jelly.

1 Place the rubber ball in the top of the bucket. Spread a thin coating of petroleum jelly over just less than half the ball's surface.

2 Tear some pieces of paper into small strips. Place some wallpaper paste into a small dish. Dip the pieces of torn paper into the paste and put them on to the ball. Make sure you cover the area of the ball's surface which has been coated with petroleum jelly. Now brush paste over the paper-covered surface of the ball and add a second layer of torn paper pieces. Make these overlap. If time permits, allow these two layers to dry. Continue to add further layers (five or six layers will be sufficient). Allow the pasted paper to dry completely.

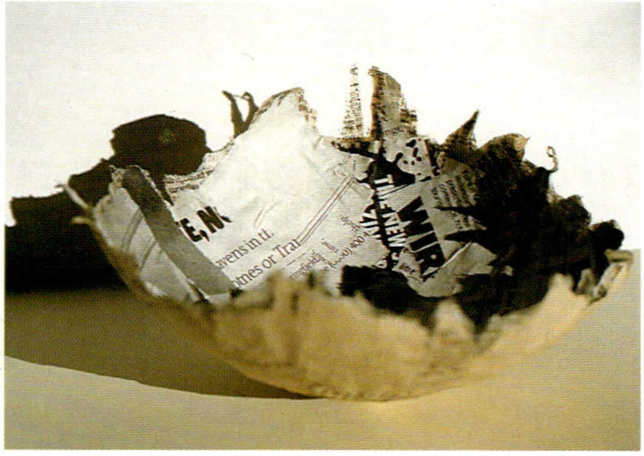

3 When the adhesive has dried out and the papier mâché bowl seems to be firm, gently remove it from the rubber ball. It will have an irregular rim. You may wish to leave this as a decorative feature, otherwise cut it with scissors to make it straighter. Decorate your bowl with painted patterns.

4 Make a papier mâché dish using a lemon (or orange) instead of a rubber ball.

5 Make a small animal from your papier mâché dish.

6 Paint in its eyes and use some string for its tail.

7 Make a papier mâché mask using a pottery bowl as your mould.

8 Paint the inside of your bowl shape blue, and trim it with a pair of scissors.

9 Paint on a face.

10 Cut strips of orange paper.

11 'Curl' the strips of paper. Hold a paper strip between your thumb and first finger and carefully pull the edge of a blunt knife or pen along the paper.

12 Fasten the curled strips to your mask with sticky tape, to represent hair.

13 The finished mask.

14 This is another simple mask. It was large enough to wear, so small holes were made in the eyes and it was held in place by a rubber band.

15 Decorate a papier mâché pot with paint.

16 After painting the inside white, add blue dribbles.

17 Formal patterns may also be used, while kitchen foil will produce different effects.

18 This delicate green and blue bowl was inspired by a bird's egg.

19 Try combining two bowls to produce a different shape.

On your own

1 Using a Stanley knife and metal ruler, cut some patterns into fairly strong paper.

2

2 and 3 These pictures will give you some pattern ideas.

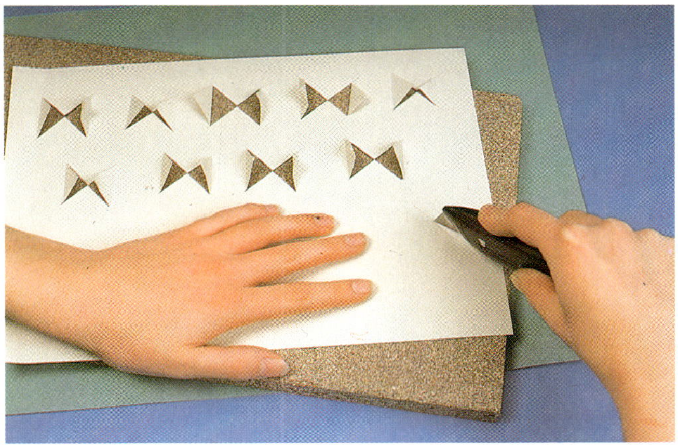

3

4 Try raising up parts of the patterns for effect.

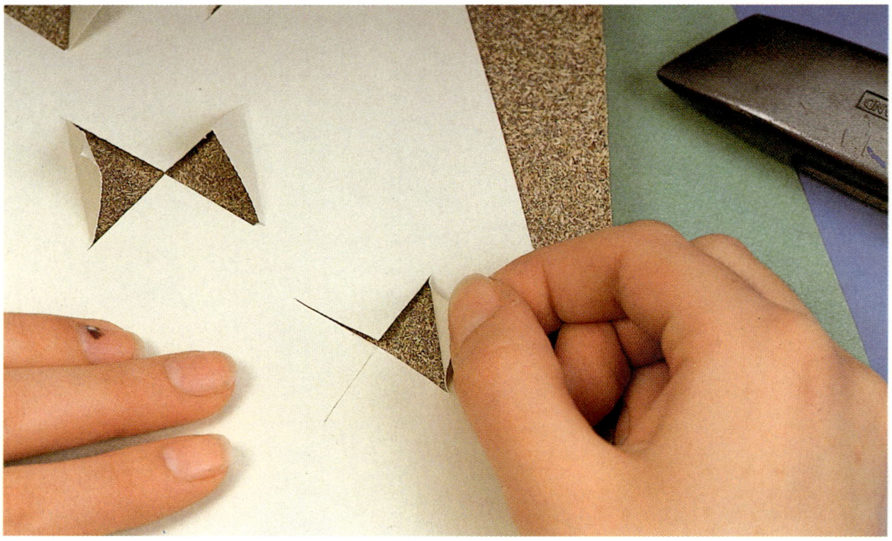

5 and **6** Why not produce simple standing structures to look like buildings or sculptures?

5

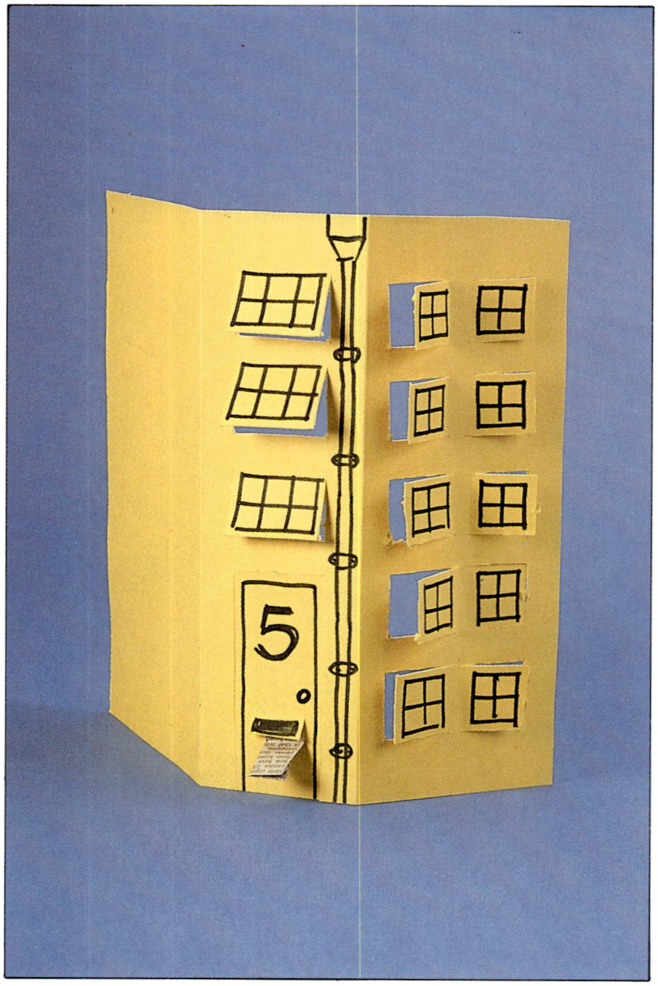

6

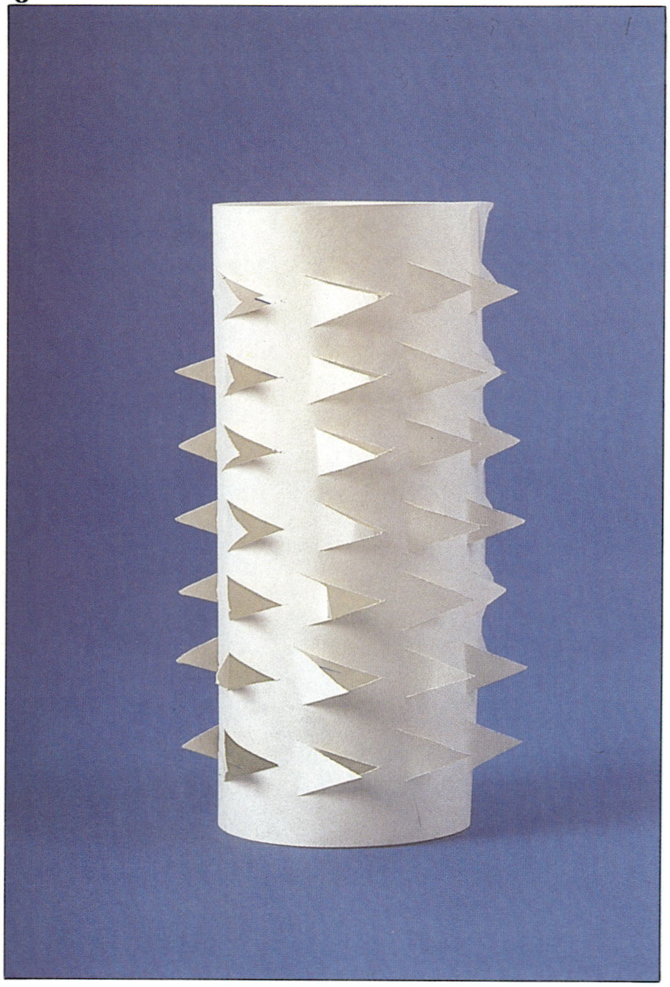

7 Make more torn paper pattern reliefs with plain white and coloured paper. Add some pieces torn from magazine photographs for effect.

8 Twist some of the paper strips to make one of your patterns different.

9 Design three cut paper patterns based upon squares.

Now go on to be much more inventive. Experiment freely. Develop some of the ideas you have already tried out. Mount your work neatly on stiff card or coloured paper and display it.

Further information

Most of the materials mentioned in this book are easy to obtain. Some are simply scrap materials and will cost you nothing. Others, such as paints, felt-tipped pens and adhesives, can be purchased from stationers and/or artists' materials shops. A visit to a DIY store will provide you with items such as wood, household paintbrushes and cheap plastic buckets. Materials in large quantities can be ordered through a schools' supplier such as E J Arnold & Sons Ltd (see below).

If you want to get a range of papers, both hand- and machine-made, you will find the following suppliers useful:

E J ARNOLD & SONS, Parkside, Dewsbury Road, Leeds LS11 5TD

BEROL, Old Meadow Road, King's Lynn, Norfolk PE30 4JR

FALKINER FINE PAPERS LTD, 76 Southampton Row, London WC1B 4AR

MANSFIELD, Jane, Greenhill House, Pentrecagal, Newcastle Emlyn, Wales

MARGROS LTD, 182 Drury Lane, London WC2

PAPYRUS, 25 Broad Street, Bath

RICHARDSON, Maureen, Romilly, Brilley, Hay-on-Wye, Hereford HR3 6HE

RUSSELL BOOK CRAFTS, Great North Road, Wyboston, Bedfordshire MK44 3AB

WINSOR & NEWTON LTD, 51 Rathbone Place, London W1

Some helpful books

HUNTER, Dard, *Papermaking: The History and Technique of an Ancient Craft*, Constable, 1978

TURNER, Silvie & SKIOLD, Birgit, *Handmade Paper Today*, Lund Humphries, 1983

HELLER, J, *Papermaking*, Watson Guptill

HOPKINSON, Anthony, *Papermaking At Home*, Thorsons, 1978

RICHARDSON, M, *Plant Papers: Handmade Papers from Garden Plants and Recycled Papers with Domestic Equipment*

SHANNON, Faith, *Paper Pleasure: From basic skills to creative ideas*, Mitchell Beazley, 1987

ROTTGER, Ernst, *Creative Paper Craft*, Batsford 1961

Index